Happy St.Patrick's Day

Everything You Need to Know about St.Patrick's Day:

(History, Meaning, Quizzes, Quotes, Puzzles, Crossword)

Copyright © 2021

All rights reserved.

DEDICATION

The author and publisher have provided this e-book to you for your personal use only. You may not make this e-book publicly available in any way. Copyright infringement is against the law. If you believe the copy of this e-book you are reading infringes on the author's copyright, please notify the publisher at: https://us.macmillan.com/piracy

Contents

History of St. Patrick's Day *1*

Meaning of St. Patrick's Day *7*

QUIZ *24*

GAME *43*

QUOTES *51*

ACKNOWLEDGMENTS

This book contains 5 parts History of St. Patrick's Day, History of St. Patrick's Day, Quiz, Game and Quotes.

St. Patrick's Day has been celebrated for centuries. But what are the holiday's origins, and who exactly was St. Patrick? Learn about the patron saint of Ireland, why St. Patrick's Day is associated with four-leafed clovers, and how the American Revolution contributed to the growth of this once minor religious holiday. The book will explain in detail for all of your questions!

This Book is ideal either as a standalone quiz, an Irish themed quiz and game on or around St Patrick's Day (17th March) with 60 Questions and Crossword Game, Word Search Puzzles.

St. Patrick's Day related quotes and feel free to forward these wonderful funny Irish quotes to your friends. It would also be a good idea to incorporate the Irish quotes and send it with a St. Patrick's Day greeting card.

Happy St. Patrick's Day

History of St. Patrick's Day

When you think of St. Patrick's Day, you probably think of green beer, shot glass necklaces that say "Kiss Me I'm Irish," and everybody talking about how Irish they suddenly are. That's all well and good, but I bet you don't know much about the holiday's origins, or the saint it celebrates. Well, take off that stupid hat, stop talking like a leprechaun for a second, and educate yourself a smidge.

St. Patrick, considered the patron saint of Ireland, was actually born in Banna Venta Berniae, a town in Roman Britain, sometime in the late 300s AD. That's right, Patrick wasn't Irish. And his name wasn't Patrick either—it was Maewyn Succat, but he didn't care for that so he chose to be known as Patricius down the line. He actually had many monikers throughout his life: he was known by many as Magonus, by others as Succetus, and to some as Cothirthiacus. But we'll just call him Patrick since everybody else does. Has a nice ring to it...

His father, Calpurnius, was a deacon in the early Christian church, but Patrick wasn't much of a believer himself. It wasn't until he was captured by Irish pirates at the age of 16 and enslaved for six years as a shepherd that he chose to convert to Christianity. While in northeastern Ireland, Patrick learned the Irish language and culture before attempting to escape back to Britain. But Patrick wasn't very good at escaping apparently, because he was captured again. This time by the French. He was held in France where he learned all about monasticism before he was released and sent home to Britain where he continued to study Christianity well into his twenties. Eventually, Patrick claimed he had a vision that told him to bring Christianity to the Irish people, who were predominantly pagan and druidic at the time, so Patrick he made his way back to Ireland and brought a big ol' bag of Christianity with him.

When Patrick arrived back in Ireland, however, he and his preaching ways were not welcomed, so he had to leave and land on some small islands off the coast. There he began to gain followers, and he eventually moved to the mainland to spread Christian ideologies across Ireland for many years to come. During this time, Patrick baptized thousands of people (some say 100,000), ordained new priests, guided women to nunhood, converted the sons of kings in the region, and aided in the formation of over 300 churches.

Folklore also tells of Patrick banishing all the snakes from Ireland, but as badass as that may sound, there were never actually any snakes on the island to begin with. Lame, I know. But Patrick may be the one responsible for popularizing the shamrock, or that three-leafed plant you'll see plastered all over the place today. According to legend, Patrick used it to teach the Irish the concept of the Christian Holy Trinity. They already had triple deities and regarded the number three highly, so Patrick's use of the shamrock may have helped him win a great deal of favor with the Irish.

These days, Patricius is known to most as Saint Patrick. Though he's not technically a canonized saint by the Catholic Church, he's well-regarded throughout the Christian world. But why the holiday? Why always March 17? What's with the green? And why do we think of a non-Irish, non-snake charmer as a symbol of Ireland?

St. Paddy's Day started as a religious celebration in the 17th century to commemorate the life of Saint Patrick and the arrival of Christianity in Ireland. This "Feast Day" always took place on the anniversary of Patrick's death, which was believed to be March 17, 461 AD. In the early 18th century, Irish immigrants brought the tradition over to the American colonies, and it was there that Saint Patrick started to become the symbol of Irish heritage and culture that he is today. As more Irish came across the Atlantic, the Feast Day celebration slowly grew in popularity. So much so, in fact, the first ever St. Patrick's Day parade was held in Boston in 1737.

By the mid 19th century, the United States saw a massive influx of Irish immigrants hoping to escape the Great Famine. This transformed the relatively small-scale Feast Day observance into a full-blown celebration that people wanted to be a part of whether they were Irish or not. In 1903, Feast Day became a national holiday in Ireland, and over time it transformed into what is now called St. Patrick's Day. The holiday has since been celebrated all over the world in countries like the United States, Great Britain, Canada, Argentina, Australia, New Zealand, Switzerland, Russia, and even throughout Asia. As it happens, St. Paddy's Day is so popular, it's thought to be celebrated in more countries than any other national festival. What was once a fairly chill day of going to mass, watching a parade, and eating a hearty meal with family has transformed into the biggest party in the world.

If you're wondering why you're wearing green right now, there's more to it than protection from pinching fingers. It goes back to the Irish Rebellion, when Irish soldiers wore green as they fought off the British in their trademark red. Until then, the color associated with St. Patrick and Feast Day was actually blue. The song soldiers sang during

Happy St. Patrick's Day

the war in 1798, "The Wearing of the Green," changed all of that and made green, the color of shamrocks, Ireland's mainstay color. From then on, people wore green on St. Patrick's Day in solidarity. And when Chicago dyed their river green for the first time in 1962, the practice of wearing and decorating in green became a part of pop culture. It's now commonplace to bust out your best greens mid-March.

Okay, so why all the drinking then? It's part historical subtext, part us succumbing to advertising, and part stereotyping. Originally, St. Patrick's Day, or Feast Day, saw the lifting of Lent restrictions for the day, giving Christians a breather as they made their way to Easter. Basically, it was a day to eat and drink as much as you please in celebration, hence the traditional Irish meal of bacon and cabbage. But imbibing on whiskey and beer was not part of the equation. In fact, pubs in Ireland were forced by law to shut down for the holiday until later in the 20th century, and drinking alcohol on St. Patrick's Day was greatly frowned upon until the late 1970s.

Then, a huge marketing push from Budweiser in the 80s convinced thirsty revelers that drinking beer and St. Patrick's Day were one in the same. The rest is drunk history nobody seems to remember, as it's all been replaced in our heads with quotes from Boondock Saints. Much like Cinco de Mayo, many people now use the holiday as an excuse to binge drink, which fosters negative stereotypes by incorrectly associating the act of getting wasted with Irish culture. But, at least now you can take a swig of your Guinness in pride because you know the real story. Sláinte!

Meaning of St. Patrick's Day

Who was Saint Patrick and Why does he have a day?

St. Paddy's Day is mostly a U.S.-based event, though cities around the world do celebrate with lots of green and lots of beer.

St. Patrick's Day has been celebrated for centuries. But what are the holiday's origins, and who exactly was St. Patrick? Learn about the patron saint of Ireland, why St. Patrick's Day is associated with four-leafed clovers, and how the American Revolution contributed to the growth of this once minor religious holiday.

St. Patrick's day is a cultural and religious holiday held annually on March 17. Named after the patron saint of Ireland, Saint Patrick, the day celebrates Irish heritage with food, parades, drinks, Irish lore, and an assortment of green-colored things—green beer, anyone?

Who was Saint Patrick?

Maewyn Succat wasn't particularly religious growing up—or even Irish, for that matter—so it's a bit surprising that he became patron saint of Ireland.

Born in Britain around A.D. 390, Maewyn grew up in a well-to-do

Christian family, complete with slaves and property. At 16, however, Maewyn was kidnapped and whisked away to Ireland where he himself became a slave and tended sheep for six or seven years; accounts differ. It was then that Maewyn became deeply religious.

Eventually, legend has it, Maewyn began to hear voices, one of which told him to escape back to Britain. He managed to gain passage on a ship, but once he reunited with his family, the voice told him to return to Ireland

Before returning, he was ordained as a priest and changed his name to Patricius, or Patrick, inspired by the Latin root "patr-" for "father."

At the time, most of Ireland was pagan and progress was hard-won by the missionary—he was often beaten and imprisoned by Irish royalty and pagan chiefs. After his death, he was largely forgotten. But then, slowly, the legend around Patrick grew until he was honored as the patron saint of Ireland.

St. Patrick's Day, the American way

St. Patrick's Day started as a minor religious holiday in 1631. The church declared it a feast day; pubs closed and observers went to church.

But the first St. Patrick's Day parade was even earlier, and in America, according to the Washington Post. Ancient Spanish documents were discovered that showed the first recorded parade in honor of St. Patrick was in St. Augustine, Florida, in 1601. Although it was a Spanish settlement, St. Patrick was regarded as the patron saint of corn in the settlement. Since those early days, the parade tradition has spread throughout the U.S. and abroad, including Ireland.

Similarly, the food most associated with the holiday—corned beef with cabbage and potatoes—also started in the United States.

During the Irish potato famine from 1845-52, nearly one million Irish emigrated to the United States. Discriminated against and poor, Irish-Americans began eating corned beef from neighboring Jewish butchers and delis. The corned beef, simmered with cabbage, turnips, or potatoes, was inexpensive and became a staple. Over time, this Irish-American tradition became closely associated with St. Patrick's Day itself, even though people in Ireland rarely ate beef.

As for the St. Patrick Day drink of choice, Guinness originated in Ireland and their flagship brew, Guinness Stout, is still brewed in their famous St. James's Gate Brewery in Dublin. St. Patrick's Day revelers consumed 13 million pints of Guinness on the holiday in 2017.

The color green The Chicago River Dyed Green

On St. Patrick's Day, cities across the world turn iconic monuments green: the Sydney Opera House, the Pyramids at Giza, and the Eiffel Tower are all lit with green lights. The Chicago River is dyed bright green. In the U.S., people who don't wear the color green on St. Patrick's Day are pinched. As Irish immigrants spread out over the United States, other cities developed their own traditions. One of these is Chicago's annual dyeing of the Chicago River green. The practice started in 1962, when city pollution-control workers used dyes to trace illegal sewage discharges and realized that the green dye might provide a unique way to celebrate the holiday

Although Chicago historians claim their city's idea for a river of green was original, some natives of Savannah, Georgia (whose St. Patrick's Day parade, the oldest in the nation, dates back to 1813) believe the idea originated in their town. They point out that, in 1961, a hotel restaurant manager named Tom Woolley convinced city officials to dye Savannah's river green. The experiment didn't exactly work as planned, and the water only took on a slight greenish hue. Savannah never attempted to dye its river again, but Woolley maintains (though others refute the claim) that he personally suggested the idea to Chicago's Mayor Richard J. Daley.

Green is the color of St. Patrick's Day, but why?

According to some scholars, the color green only became associated with Ireland and St. Patrick's Day during the Irish Rebellion in 1798. Before then, Ireland was known for the color blue since it featured prominently in the royal court and on ancient Irish flags.

During the rebellion against Britain, however, Irish soldiers chose to wear green—the color that most contrasted the red British uniforms—and sang, "The Wearing of the Green." This firmly established the link between Ireland and the color green.

St. Patrick's Day Celebrations Around the World

Today, people of all backgrounds celebrate St. Patrick's Day, especially throughout the United States, Canada and Australia. Although North America is home to the largest productions, St. Patrick's Day is celebrated in many other locations far from Ireland, including Japan, Singapore and Russia.

In modern-day Ireland, St. Patrick's Day was traditionally been a religious occasion. In fact, up until the 1970s, Irish laws mandated that pubs be closed on March 17. Beginning in 1995, however, the Irish government began a national campaign to use interest in St. Patrick's Day to drive tourism and showcase Ireland and Irish culture to the rest of the world. Approximately 1 million people annually take part in Ireland 's St. Patrick's Festival in Dublin, a multi-day celebration featuring parades, concerts, outdoor theater productions and fireworks shows.

Facts About St. Patrick's Day

1. St Patrick was born in 385 AD in a place believed to be Banna Venta Berniae, a town in Roman Britain (his exact place of birth is however uncertain). He died during the fifth century in the year 461 AD at Saul, Downpatrick, Ireland.

2. St Patrick's Day commemorates the arrival of the Christianity in Ireland. It happened in the year 432.

3. Patrick was born to Roman parents (Calpurnius and Conchessa). He was not Irish, instead, he was English. His given name was Maewyn Succat. Thus, technically we would be celebrating "Maewyn Day" instead of the "St Patrick's Day" if his name was not changed. He wrote a book–Confessio–during his last years.

4. At the age of 16, St Patrick was kidnapped and was taken to Ireland. He was kidnapped by a group of Irish raiders who were attacking his family's estate. He worked there for 6 years tending sheep and then escaped and became a priest.

5. St Patrick's Day is also known as the 'Feast of Saint Patrick' and the 'Day of the Festival of Patrick'. Patrick studied and received his

training in the religion for more than 12 years after he escaped from the captivity of the Irish raiders.

6. Saint Patrick used Shamrock (a young sprig of clover) to teach the pagans about the Holy Trinity. The shamrock is now the official flower of Ireland. It is associated with St Patrick.

7. St Patrick's Day has been observed by the Irish as a religious holiday for more than 1,000 years.

8. 'Blue' was the color associated with St Patrick before the adoption of green as the color for the festival. The color blue was featured both in the royal court and on ancient Irish flags. In 1798, the color green became officially associated with the day.

9. The first Patrick's Day parade was held in Waterford (the oldest and the fifth most populous city in the Republic of Ireland) in 1903.

10. More than 100 Saint Patrick parades are held across the United States. Almost 12% of Americans claim Irish ancestry. More people of Irish ancestry live in the United States than in Ireland.

11. One claim in history deeply associated with St Patrick is that he banished all the snake from Ireland. However, this claim is not true

because it has been discovered that the chances of survival of snakes in Ireland are minimal because of the cold conditions of the region. However, some say that the snakes represent the pagans he converted to Christianity.

12. In 1762, the first New York City parade took place. With over 150,000 participants, the St Patricks Day parade in New York is the world's oldest civilian parade and the largest in the United States. And more than 3 million spectators line the parade route which is 1.5 miles long. The parade takes more than 5 hours to come to an end.

13. On this day, Catholics attend church in the morning and then watch a St Patrick's Day parade.

14. The Chicago River (the system of rivers and canals has a combined length of 156 miles) is dyed green on this day (since 1962). However, the first year when the river was dyed green, 100 pounds of vegetable dye was released into the river. This kept the river green for almost a week. However, today, they use only 40 lbs of the green dye to color the river for the day to keep the environmental damages in check. Now, the dye lasts for about 5 hours.

15. Guinness (an Irish dark beer that originated in the brewery of

Arthur Guinness) sale almost doubles on St Patrick's Day as compared to the regular days when 5.5 million pints of it is sold.

16. The 200th anniversary of St Patrick's Day was marked in Sydney Opera House by making it green.

17. The first St Patrick's Day celebration in the United States was held in Boston in 1737.

18. On this day, people usually eat corned beef and cabbage, and they wear green. However, corned beef is an English dish and not Irish.

19. Wearing green attire or shamrock is also a St Patrick's Day tradition. It is one of Irish tradition to pinch someone who is not wearing green on the day.

20. Between 1903 and 1970 most pubs in Ireland were closed because St Patrick's Day was a religious holiday. However, the holiday was reclassified as a national holiday and the nation started drinking even on this day. Drinking on this day has become a strong St Patrick's Day tradition.

21. St Patrick's Day is a national holiday in both Ireland and North Ireland. It is a provincial holiday in the Canadian province of

Newfoundland.

22. World's shortest St Patrick's Day parade is held in Arkansas, which runs for a total of 98 feet.

23. More than 450 churches are named for St Patrick in the United States. And 5.5 million tourists visit St. Patrick's Cathedral in New York City every year.

24. St Patrick's Day is one of the most celebrated festivals in the world. Others may include La Tomatina — Buñol, Spain; Holi — Celebrated by Hindus Around the World; Carnaval — Rio de Janeiro, Brazil; Lantern Festival — Pingxi, Taiwan.

25. St Patrick's Day parades began in North America in the 17th century but they did not spread to Ireland until the 20th century.

26. St Patrick's Day is not celebrated on March 17 when it falls within the Holy Week (the week just before Easter, Holy Week in 2018 will begin on Sunday, 25 March and ends on Saturday, 31 March). This once happened when the day coincided with Palm Sunday in 1940 and then again in 2008. The celebration of the Day is adjusted in such a scenario. In 1940 it was observed on 3 April and in 2008 it was

observed on 15 March. Now, until 2160, St Patrick's Day will not fall under the Holy Week.

27. St Patrick's Day is celebrated in countries including Canada, Australia, Japan, Singapore, Russia and other countries of the Irish Diaspora (refers to Irish people and their descendants who live outside Ireland).

28. More than 1 million people take part in the St Patrick's Festival (between March 15th and 17th) in Dublin every year.

29. John F Kennedy the 35th president of the United States of America worn a green tie for photographs when Ireland's ambassador to the US, Thomas Kiernan, turned up at the White House with a bowl of shamrock on 17 March.

30. Finding a four leaf clover on St Patrick's Day is considered lucky as you only have one chance in 10,000. Generally, you will find a three leaf clover.

31. We Should Really Wear Blue

Saint Patrick himself would have to deal with pinching on his feast day. His color was "Saint Patrick's blue," a light shade. The color green only became associated with the big day after it was linked to the Irish independence movement in the late 18th century.

32. Saint Patrick Was British

Although he made his mark by introducing Christianity to Ireland in the year 432, Patrick wasn't Irish himself. He was born to Roman parents in Scotland or Wales in the late fourth century.

33. The Irish Take Saint Patrick's Day Seriously

As you might expect, Saint Patrick's Day is a huge deal in his old stomping grounds. It's a national holiday in both Ireland and Northern Ireland.

34. So Do New Yorkers

New York City's Saint Patrick's Day Parade is one of the world's largest parades. Since 1762, 250,000 marchers have traipsed up Fifth Avenue on foot – the parade still doesn't allow floats, cars, or other modern trappings.

35. Chicago Feels Lucky, Too

New York may have more manpower, but Chicago has a spectacle all its own. The city has been celebrating Saint Patrick by dumping green dye into the Chicago River since 1962. It takes 40 tons of dye to get the river to a suitably festive shade!

36. It Used to Be a Dry Holiday

For most of the 20th century, Saint Patrick's Day was considered a strictly religious holiday in Ireland, which meant that the nation's pubs were closed for business on March 17. (The one exception went to beer vendors at the big national dog show, which was always held on Saint Patrick's Day.) In 1970, the day was converted to a national holiday, and the stout resumed flowing.

37. It's the Thought That Counts

Not every city goes all-out in its celebratory efforts. From 1999 to 2007, the Irish village of Dripsey proudly touted that it hosted the Shortest Saint Patrick's Day Parade in the World. The route ran for 26 yards between two pubs. Today, Hot Springs, Arkansas claims the title for brevity – its brief parade runs for 98 feet.

38. There's a Reason for The Shamrocks

How did the shamrock become associated with Saint Patrick? According to Irish legend, the saint used the three-leafed plant as a metaphor for the Holy Trinity when he was first introducing Christianity to Ireland.

39. Cold Weather Helped Saint Patrick's Legend

In Irish lore, Saint Patrick gets credit for driving all the snakes out of Ireland. Modern scientists suggest that the job might not have been too hard – according to the fossil record, Ireland has never been home to any snakes. Through the Ice Age, Ireland was too cold to host any reptiles, and the surrounding seas have staved off serpentine invaders ever since. Modern scholars think the "snakes" Saint Patrick drove away were likely metaphorical.

40. There's No Corn in that Beef

Corned beef and cabbage, a traditional Saint Patrick's Day staple, doesn't have anything to do with the grain corn. Instead, it's a nod to the large grains of salt that were historically used to cure meats, which were also known as "corns."

41. The World Runs Up Quite a Bar Tab

All of the Saint Patrick's Day revelry around the globe is great news for brewers. A 2012 estimate pegged the total amount spent on beer for Saint Patrick's Day celebrations at $245 million. And that's before tips to pubs' bartenders.

42. It Could have Been Saint Maewyn's Day

According to Irish legend, Saint Patrick wasn't originally called Patrick. His birth name was Maewyn Succat, but he changed his name to Patricius after becoming a priest.

43. There Are No Female Leprechauns

Don't be fooled by any holiday decorations showing lady leprechauns. In traditional Irish folk tales, there are no female leprechauns, only nattily attired little guys.

44. But the Leprechaun Economy Is Thriving

Another little-known fact from Irish lore: Leprechauns earned that gold they're guarding. According to legend, leprechauns spend their days making and mending shoes. It's hard work, so you can't blame them for being territorial about their pots of gold.

45. The Lingo Makes Sense

You can't attend a Saint Patrick's Day event without hearing a cry of "Erin go Bragh." What's the phrase mean? It's a corruption of the Irish Éirinn go Brách, which means roughly "Ireland Forever."

Happy St.Patrick's Day

QUIZ

1. People traditionally wear green on St. Patrick's Day to avoid what?

   A. Getting Kissed

   B. Getting Pinched

   C. One Year Back Luck

   D. People Not Knowing They're Irish

2. What nationality was St. Patrick?

   A. Irish

   B. German

   C. Scottish

   D. British

3. What did St. Patrick believe a shamrock represented?

   A. Good Luck

   B. Good Fortune

   C. The Holy Trinity

   D. Nature

4. Which U.S. city dyes its river green annually to celebrate St. Patrick's Day?

A. Boston

B. Detroit

C. Chicago

D. New York City

5. According to myth, when is the best time to sneak up on a leprechaun?

A. When he's taking a nap

B. When he's counting gold

C. While he's mending his shoes

D. When he's eating

6. What was St. Patrick's given birth name?

A. Henry O'Malley

B. Patrick O'Riley

C. Gabriel McSweeney

D. Maewyn Succat

7. How many pints of Guinness are consumed worldwide on St. Patrick's Day?

A. 13 Million

B. 1 Million

C. 6 Million

D. 1 Billion

8. Which of the following colors are in the Irish flag?

   A. White, Green & Yellow

   B. Yellow, Orange & White

   C. Green, Yellow & Orange

   D. Green, White & Orange

9. Myth says that if a human catches a leprechaun, he has the ability to do what in turn for his release?

   A. Give you his shoes

   B. Grant three wishes

   C. Reveal the secret to life

   D. Lead you to his gold

10. Which of these colors was originally associated with St. Patrick's Day?

    A. Orange

    B. Blue

Happy St. Patrick's Day

C. White

D. Green

Happy St.Patrick's Day

Answer - 1 B

Answer - 2 C

Answer - 3 C

Answer - 4 C

Answer - 5 C

Answer - 6 D

Answer - 7 A

Answer - 8 D

Answer - 9 B

Answer - 10   B

Happy St.Patrick's Day

11. St. Patrick is the patron saint of ___.

    A. England

    B. France

    C. Ireland

12. St. Patrick's Day is celebrated on ___.

    A. February 14th

    B. March 17th

    C. December 25th

13. In New York city a huge ___ is held to celebrate St. Patrick's Day.

    A. parade

    B. marathon

    C. demonstration

14. A ___ strip is painted down the centre of 5th avenue.

    A. yellow

    B. red

    C. green

Happy St.Patrick's Day

15. Millions of Shamrocks are flown from Ireland. A shamrock is a small plant with ___ leaves.

    A. one

    B. two

    C. three

    D. four

16. Green is the colour that ___ the Irish people.

    A. indicates

    B. suggests

    C. represents

17. St. Patrick's Day is celebrated on the day that Patrick ___.

    A. got married

    B. was born

    C. died

18. A well known story about him says that he drove all the ___ out of Ireland.

    A. snakes

    B. bears

C. women

19. Many famous politicians including President ___ are of Irish descent.

    A. Nixon

    B. Clinton

    C. Kennedy

20. St. Patrick was born in ___.

    A. England

    B. Ireland

    C. the U.S.A.

    Answer - 11   C

    Answer - 12   B

    Answer - 13   A

    Answer - 14   C

    Answer - 15   C

    Answer - 16   C

    Answer - 17   C

Happy St.Patrick's Day

Answer - 18   A

Answer - 19   C

Answer - 20   A

21. St. Patrick's Day is celebrated to commemorate which of the following events?

A. It is the day St. Patrick died

22. Which one of the following you know as the day St Patrick died?

A. March 17, AD 461

23. Where was St. Patrick born?

A. Britain

24. Which of the following is NOT associated with St. Patrick's Day?

A. Purple

25. What does the shamrock signify on the Day?

A. A fairy

26. What does leperchaun mean?

A. Number 3

27. Which of the following is most likely to come up in your traditional St. Patrick's Day party?

A. Potato

28. Where does Blarney Stone come from?

A. A castle

29. When were the customs of the St. Patrick's Day brought in America?

A. 1737

30. Which of the following was the first to officially celebrate the Day?

A. Boston

31. Which of the following is the language of Ireland?

A. Irish

32. Which one is regarded as the most famous of all churches dedicated to St. Patrick?

A. Dublin

33.	Which of the following activities is NOT common on St. Pat's Day?

A.	Wild party

34.	Where in US the St. Patrick's Day is celebrated by an attempt to color a river green?

A. Chicago

35.	Which of the following is NOT an Irish born?

A. Roger Moore

36.	In Ireland, what does the color green stand for?

A. Hope

37.	What colors are on the Irish flag?

A.	Green, White, Orange

38.	What was St. Patrick's calling?

A.	Missionary

Happy St. Patrick's Day

39. What do Irish people say about Saint Patrick?

   A. Both of the above

40. What is a shillelagh?

   A. Short, stout

41. According to legend, what should you never do if you catch a leprechaun?

   A. Take your eyes off him

42. What was St. Patrick's name at birth?

   A. Maewyn Succat

43. Which American city holds the largest St. Patrick's Day parade?

   A. New York

44. What profession does the leprechaun supposedly practice?

   A. Shoemaker

45. What is cured by kissing The Blarney Stone?

A. Shyness

46. What does "Erin Go Braugh" mean?

A. Ireland forever

47. Who kidnapped Maewyn Succat?

A. A band of pirates

48. How long did St Patrick's mission in Ireland last?

A. 30 years

49. What happens if you don't wear green on St. Patrick's Day?

A. You get pinched

50. If you catch a Leprechaun and take your eyes off him, what happens?

A. He vanishes

Happy St.Patrick's Day

51. St.Patrick was born in Ireland. True or False?

A. True
B. False

52. St.Patrick's Day is March 17. What does this date commemorate?

A. his becoming bishop of Ireland
B. his birth
C. his death
D. his conversion to Christianity

53. Why did Patrick go to Ireland?

A. his parents took him
B. he was shipwrecked there

C. he liked to see new places

D. he was taken by pirates

54. After six years he left Ireland and went to this country.

A. Italy

B. England

C. Scotland

D. France

55. He became a monk and later returned to Ireland. What did he return to Ireland as?

A. shepherd

B. bishop

C. chieftan

D. pedlar

Happy St.Patrick's Day

56. How many churches was St.Patrick supposed to have founded?

A. 90
B. 25
C. 300
D. 150

57. What did Saint Patrick use to illustrate the Trinity, and which later became a symbol of Ireland?

58. A legend says that St.Patrick rid Ireland of these creatures.

A. rats
B. trolls
C. snakes
D. leprechauns

Happy St.Patrick's Day

59. When was the first St.Patrick's Day parade held in New York City?

A. 1862
B. 1662
C. 1962
D. 1762

60. The color associated with St.Patrick's Day and with Ireland is green. What green nickname does Ireland go by?

Answer - 51   B

Answer - 52   C

Answer - 53   D

Answer - 54   D

Happy St.Patrick's Day

Answer - 55   B

Answer - 56   C

Answer - 57   Sharmrok

Answer - 58   C

Answer - 59   D

Answer - 60   Emerald Isle

Happy St.Patrick's Day

GAME

St. Patrick's Day Word Search Puzzle

O	R	L	E	P	R	E	C	H	A	U	N	I	A	P
U	S	P	T	L	S	W	W	P	O	T	Y	U	W	V
J	P	A	R	I	H	U	B	C	N	S	A	I	N	T
L	A	T	A	M	A	H	L	S	S	F	A	I	R	Y
B	R	R	I	E	M	C	E	I	R	E	L	A	N	D
L	T	I	N	R	R	L	S	P	P	A	R	A	D	E
C	Y	C	B	I	O	O	S	S	N	A	K	E	S	A
P	M	K	O	C	C	V	I	U	Z	B	N	K	B	M
L	L	X	W	K	K	E	N	J	V	L	P	O	C	U
L	E	P	Z	P	A	R	G	T	U	A	I	H	T	O
U	A	N	K	M	A	G	I	C	U	R	W	R	D	L
C	W	I	S	H	T	R	K	B	A	N	C	U	X	K
K	E	C	V	M	G	R	E	E	N	G	O	L	D
Y	V	E	M	E	R	A	L	D	R	Y	T	A	I	B
C	U	X	M	A	R	C	H	Y	I	R	I	S	H	V

Word List

SAINT
PATRICK
IRISH
BLARNEY
BLESSING
EMERALD
LEPRECHAUN
GOLD
GREEN
IRELAND
LIMERICK
MAGIC
PARADE
RAINBOW
SHAMROCK
LUCKY
WISH
FAIRY
MARCH
PARTY
CLOVER
POT
SNAKES

Search the puzzle for the words shown in the word list. Circle each word that you find until you find all of the words in the whole puzzle!

43

Happy St.Patrick's Day

Happy St.Patrick's Day

St. Patrick's Day Crossword

Down:
1: The official language of Ireland (along with English)
2: What St. Patrick banished from Ireland
3: Symbol of good luck
4: 3 leaved green supposedly eaten to freshen breath in the 1600's
5: The _____ Isle
6: A custom or belief passed down through generations
7: Country where St. Patrick's Day started
8: Color associated most with St. Patrick's Day
9: Color of coins
10: Language group that includes Irish and Scottish
11: Humorous verse consisting of 3 long lines and 2 short lines

Across:
12: What happens if you don't wear green; you get _____
13: Small, mischievous spirit
14: Major US city that dyes river green for St. Patrick's Day
15: What you follow to get to the pot of gold
16: Capital of Ireland
17: Day of the month that St. Patrick's Day falls on
18: Month that St. Patrick's Day is in
19: Having good luck
20: What you find at the end of the rainbow; _____ of gold

Happy St.Patrick's Day

St. Patrick's Day

Across
1. A mischievous elf in Irish Folklore
4. A branch of the Indo-European languages that was spread widely over Europe in the pre-Christian era.
7. To publicly party
8. The Celtic language of Ireland
12. A plant of the genus Trifolium
13. March in a procession
15. Something likened to the metal in brightness or preciousness
16. A month of a year
18. Resembling the color of growing grass
20. An occasion on which people can assemble for social interaction and entertainment
21. A staple food of Ireland
22. Occurring by chance
24. A story about mythical or supernatural beings or events
25. An inherited pattern of thought or action
26. Another word for 3-leaf clover

Down
2. Invoke upon
3. A humorous verse form of 5 anapestic lines with a rhyme scheme aabba.
5. A special kind of clover
6. Christian missionary and bishop in Ireland
9. Any art that invokes supernatural powers
10. Achieved independence from the UK in 1921
11. An arc of colored light in the sky caused by refraction of the sun's rays by rain
14. The day of the month of St Patrick's day
17. A small being, human in form, playful and having magical powers
19. Highly valued as a gemstone
23. A form of money

Happy St. Patrick's Day

Saint Patrick's Day

ACROSS

1. According to legend, at the end of a rainbow you will find a pot of _____
5. St. Patrick's Day is generally celebrated in the month of _____
6. Irish celtic music is usually played with this instrument
7. St. Patrick's Day is the national holiday of which country?
9. Another name for a three leaf clover that Saint Patrick used to explain the holy trinity
10. Which color is usually seen on this holiday?

DOWN

2. This make-believe character is always searching for his pot of gold
3. Many cities have a _____ in the street to celebrate St. Patrick's Day
4. One of the most popular foods for St. Patrick's Day is Corned Beef and _____
8. When the Great Potato Famine of 1845 hit Ireland, almost one million Irish people moved to _____

WORD BANK: America, bagpipe, cabbage, gold, green, ireland, leprechaun, march, parade, shamrock.

47

Happy St. Patrick's Day

ST. PATRICK'S DAY CROSSWORD PUZZLE

ACROSS

3. An Irish club that doubles as a walking stick
5. Christmas in ___ with all of the folks at home
7. Irish native language
8. Ancient culture of Ireland
10. Ireland forever!
11. Capital city of Ireland
12. Found at the end of a rainbow

DOWN

1. Practical jokes
2. Used by St. Patrick to represent the Christian Trinity
4. Tricky elf-like creature who jealousy guards his pot of gold
6. Patron saint of Ireland
7. Ireland has forty shades of ___
9. When Irish eyes are ___

Happy St. Patrick's Day

St. Patrick's Day Word Puzzle

```
              I C E L T I C W           A J O S U I P L
            Z Z L U C K L U I D       U U G B H X L Q T T
            S S N D T A E K Y B M   G U O W J E U O M F F
        N N   R T V N T N V A B C   O G F C M N C Z W V   W U
      V I A U   E S L S L T K P U   L K X J E A O S T   Q E I I
      K R V L R P P G V T D M T Q   D V J C X N R X T Z W N A N
      G M Z F S A F I Z G P D Q L   R F D K A I O L R H K P A C
      T Z H O W P I D P H H A W O   E E M N D G N Z E C C L T M
      N B J G M S N N N G E G T L   E W E W P A A T A R A B V F
      I A F Y R V E U B R A T K R   L V S B I N T A S U B S Q A
      A G M A G S U I G O W B A V I H I W S E S I A U H B Z I E
      S I X C I R I S H V W N X R J C B X G D Q O Y R C A R L L
        P X C O Y S W A W L I U I B L K I I R H N Y E P G O S
          L C E K E G X L A Q P A A E O H H J D S Z U L E O
                        N J I R H O L H I
              N V D V F E U U F A N M I C R E D G D A N C E G W
            K P D K X I Z M I L E R Q F D E F C M P G M V G G P N
          K C O R M A H S C E Y K U Z A C X R T N E T D O T D P P G
          N Y M S J I G H N S R V O P E F P F P D Z L M X N S M A D
          E N H G W V A C T A T A F Y   L E B V E F J C D Y E K R H
          E R T T W R O O R A D I L P   O M X L N L I Z U N K I A S
          R V G K M B N W U I G R H D   K S X H B O R T S I A P D I
          G I Q Q N E J W H Y E W P C   F S Q M C C E A T F N O E I
          M O Z O Z X M X W V R Q O L   Z I D C T R L Z Y W S T P B
          F G N H   L S R O E L I U T   U K M H M R A Z E   G T M X
            G J     L Q X L Z L G B A N   O M S A Y V N M Q Q   G K
                X V Q C X M I I K X F   Z L O O H S D F G S A
                  S M E P R A H S L R   U Z B J Q H D J K P
                    C X B L E A M V     Z H E D X C I V
```

Word List:

BAGPIPERS	CLOVER	IRELAND	POT
BEER	CORONATION	IRISH	RAINBOW
BLARNEYSTONE	DANCE	JIG	SAINT
CABBAGE	EMERALD	KISSME	SHAMROCK
CELEBRATE	FAIRY	LEAF	SHENANIGANS
CELTIC	FOUR	LEPRECHAUN	SNAKES
CHARM	GOLD	LUCK	STPATRICK
CHURCH	GREEN	MARCH	TREASURE
CLANS	HARP	PARADE	

Happy St.Patrick's Day

St Patricks Day Word Search

Q	B	G	R	E	E	N	F	S	K	G	T	U	J	Y
S	E	V	L	E	D	T	E	T	L	H	B	P	A	H
C	N	I	H	X	Y	A	D	C	Y	O	R	H	S	N
T	Q	T	B	C	U	E	R	Z	L	B	T	H	H	W
K	L	E	P	R	E	C	H	A	U	N	A	Z	V	H
R	S	K	K	O	E	H	U	U	P	M	G	O	K	W
T	H	Z	L	B	W	R	U	H	R	G	T	C	O	N
H	H	N	X	H	J	J	O	O	O	W	I	B	V	G
A	C	F	T	R	B	T	C	P	A	R	N	T	M	Y
T	R	R	T	Z	D	K	A	L	T	I	M	E	Z	K
G	A	T	S	B	S	Z	I	A	A	H	P	Z	L	L
P	M	S	I	S	V	K	P	R	Z	K	O	A	W	O
F	P	B	R	P	O	T	O	F	G	O	L	D	A	F
S	D	O	I	Z	S	O	J	F	Q	N	Y	B	I	D
K	N	O	F	A	L	P	I	B	V	B	V	G	N	Z

GREEN
SHAMROCKS
HAT
LEPRECHAUN
MARCH
RAINBOW
POTOFGOLD
ELVES
STPATRICK
PARADE

QUOTES

Quotes can at times be an effective medium through wish one can show one's mindful thoughts and feelings. See more ideas about Irish quotes. Get in the true spirit of being a true Irish and go through these reflective thoughts which will enhance the spirit of being a true Irish further. So keep on reading these St. Patrick's Day related quotes and feel free to forward these wonderful funny Irish quotes to your friends. It would also be a good idea to incorporate the Irish quotes and send it with a St. Patrick's Day greeting card.

Happy St.Patrick's Day

1. An Irishman has an abiding sense of tragedy which sustains him through temporary periods of joy. ~ Irish saying

2. The Irish forgive their great men when they are safely buried. ~ Irish saying

3. Anyone acquainted with Ireland knows that the morning of St. Patrick's Day consists of the night of the seventeenth of March flavored strongly with the morning of the eighteenth. ~ Unknown

4. St. Patrick's Day Quotes on Irish Blessing

5. May your blessings outnumber
   The shamrocks that grow,
   And may trouble avoid you
   Wherever you go. ~ Irish blessing

6. Never iron a four-leaf clover, because you don't want to press your luck. ~ Unknown

7. A best friend is like a four leaf clover: hard to find and lucky to have. ~ Unknown

8. The list of Irish saints is past counting; but in it all no other figure is so human, friendly, and lovable as St. Patrick – who was an Irishman only by adoption. ~ Stephen Gwynn

9. May the Irish hills caress you.
   May her lakes and rivers bless you.
   May the luck of the Irish enfold you.
   May the blessings of Saint Patrick behold you.
   ~ Irish blessing

Happy St.Patrick's Day

10.   Oh, the music in the air!
An' the joy that's ivrywhere -
Shure, the whole blue vault of heaven is wan grand triumphal arch,
An' the earth below is gay
Wid its tender green th'-day,
Fur the whole world is Irish on the Seventeenth o' March!
~ Thomas Augustin Daly

11.   When Irish eyes are smiling, sure 'tis like a morn in spring.
In the lilt of Irish laughter you can hear the angels sing,
When Irish hearts are happy all the world seems bright and gay,
And when Irish eyes are smiling, sure, they steal your heart away.
~ Chauncey Olcott and George Graff, Jr. (lyrics), Ernest R. Ball (music)

12.   For 'tis green, green, green, where the ruined towers are gray,
And it's green, green, green, all the happy night and day;

Green of leaf and green of sod, green of ivy on the wall,

And the blessed Irish shamrock with the fairest green of all.

13.   ~ Mary Elizabeth Blake

14.   St. Patrick's Day Quotes on Gentle Irish Ground

15.   What color should be seen

Where our fathers' homes have been

But their own immortal Green?

16.   ~ Author Unknown

17.   Oh! St. Patrick was a gentleman

Who came of decent people;

He built a church in Dublin town,

And on it put a steeple.

~ Henry Bennett

18.   May the saddest day of your future be no worse than the happiest day of your past. ~ Irish saying

19.   Here's to you and yours and to mine and ours. And if mine and ours ever come across to you and yours, I hope you and yours will do as much for mine and ours as mine and ours have done for you and yours! ~ Irish toast

20.   May you live as long as you want and never want as long as you live. ~ Irish saying

21.   St. Patrick's Day Quotes on voices from the Irish seas

22.   Drink is the curse of the land. It makes you fight with your neighbor. It makes you shoot at your landlord-and it makes you miss him. ~ Irish saying

23. A best friend is like a four leaf clover: hard to find and lucky to have. ~ Unknown

24. The list of Irish saints is past counting; but in it all no other figure is so human, friendly, and lovable as St. Patrick – who was an Irishman only by adoption. ~ Stephen Gwynn

25. St. Patrick... one of the few saints whose feast day presents the opportunity to get determinedly whacked and make a fool of oneself all under the guise of acting Irish. ~ Charles M. Madigan

26. Leprechauns, castles, good luck and laughter
Lullabies, dreams, and love ever after.
Poems and songs with pipes and drums
A thousand welcomes when anyone comes.
~ Author Unknown

27. The shamrock is forbid by law to grow on Irish ground;

28. St. Patrick's Day no more we'll keep, his colours can't be seen,

For there's a bloody law against the wearing of the green.

~ Dion Bouicault

29. There's a dear little plant that grows in our Isle,

'Twas Saint Patrick himself sure that set it;

And the sun on his labor with pleasure did smile,

And with dew from his eye often wet it.

It shines thro' the bog thro' the brake, thro' the mireland,

And he called it the dear little Shamrock of Ireland.

~ Andrew Sherry

30. When law can stop the blades of grass from growing as they grow,

And when the leaves in summer-time their verdure dare not show,

Then will I change the color that I wear in my caubeen

But 'till that day, please God, I'll stick to wearing of the green.
~ Dion Bouicault

31. St. Patrick's Day Quotes on shamrock takes the heart

32. There are many good reasons for drinking,
One has just entered my head.
If a man doesn't drink when he's living,
How in the hell can he drink when he's dead?
~ Irish saying

33. If you're lucky enough to be Irish... you're lucky enough!
~ Irish saying

34. May your thoughts be as glad as the shamrocks. May your heart be as light as a song. May each day bring you bright, happy hours. That stay with you all the year long.

~ Irish blessing

35.   No one should ever say that it was my ignorance if I did or showed forth anything however small according to God's good pleasure; but let this be your conclusion and let it so be thought, that - as is the perfect truth - it was the gift of God.
~ Saint Patrick

36.   Before I was humiliated I was like a stone that lies in deep mud, and he who is mighty came and in his compassion raised me up and exalted me very high and placed me on the top of the wall.
~ Saint Patrick

37.   "If it was raining soup, the Irish would go out with forks."
– Brendan Behan

38.   "You cannot conquer Ireland. You cannot extinguish the

Irish passion for freedom. If our deed has not been sufficient to win freedom, then our children will win by a better deed."

— Patrick Henry Pearse

39.　"Every St. Patrick's Day every Irishman goes out to find another Irishman to make a speech to." — Shane Leslie

40.　"Irish history stretches back into the dark days of the Celts, yet there is a light, laughter and a sense of laissez-faire in the Irish men and women of today."

— Richard Benson

41.　"The list of Irish saints is passing counting; but in it all no other figure is so human, friendly, and lovable as St. Patrick."

— Stephen Gwynn

42. "St. Patrick's Day is an enchanted time – a day to begin transforming winter's dreams into summer's magic."

– Adrienne Cook

43. "Oh, Paddy, dear, an' did ye hear the news that's goin' round? The shamrock is forbid by law to grow on Irish ground! No more St. Patrick's Day we'll keep, his colour can't be seen, For there's a cruel law agin' the Wearin' o' the green."

– Anonymous

44. "May your thoughts be as glad as the shamrocks. May your heart be as light as a song. May each day bring you bright, happy hours. That stay with you all the year long."

– Irish Blessing

45. "That's what the holidays are for – for one person to tell the stories and another to dispute them. Isn't that the Irish way?"

– Lara Flynn Boyle

46. "Grant me a sense of humor, Lord, the saving grace to see a joke, to win some happiness from life, and pass it on to other folks."

– Irish Prayer

47. "Ireland is a land of poets and legends, of dreamers and rebels." – Nora Roberts

48. "May St. Patrick guard you wherever you go, and guide you in whatever you do and may his loving protection be a blessing to you always."

– Irish Blessing

49. "If you hold a four-leaf shamrock in your left hand at dawn on St. Patrick's Day you get what you want very much but haven't wished for."

— Patricia Lynch

50. "Ireland has one of the world's heaviest rainfalls. If you see an Irishman with a tan, it's rust." — Dave Allen

51. "St. Patrick's Day is a day to celebrate our green heritage. The ancestry of Ireland. It is a day to celebrate what it means to be Irish and of Irish descent."

— Anthony T. Hicks

52. "Ireland is the only place in the world where procrastination takes on a sense of urgency."

— Dave Allen

53. "If you're Irish, it doesn't matter where you are – you'll find family." – Victoria Smurfit

54. "This microscopic nation in the Atlantic has little economic or political clout in the world. But somehow, Ireland's influence seems to pop up everywhere, whether you prefer to travel in the realms of high or low culture."
– Robert Sullivan

55. "Whenever I want to know what the Irish are thinking, I look into my own heart."
– Eamon de Valera

56. "May your day be touched by a bit of Irish luck, brightened by a song in your heart and warmed by the smiles of the people you love." – Irish Saying

57. "Whether I drink often, or just once in a while; I'm always sure to raise a glass to the dear old Emerald Isle." – Pat Maloney

58. "May your blessings outnumber the shamrocks that grow. And may trouble avoid you wherever you go." - Irish Blessing

59. For the whole world is Irish on the Seventeenth o' March! - Thomas Augustine Daly

60. The best luck of all is the luck you make for yourself. - Douglas McArthur

Happy St. Patrick's Day

Made in the USA
Las Vegas, NV
15 February 2022